STUDY ON SUSTAINABILITY MANAGEMENT

EVALUATION OF ORGANIZATIONAL SUSTAINABILITY METRICS (A CASE ON NIKE)

MS. CHITRITA BANERJEE

Clever Fox®
PUBLISHING
Chennai • Bangalore

CLEVER FOX PUBLISHING
Chennai, India

Published by CLEVER FOX PUBLISHING 2025

ISBN: 978-93-6707-420-6

प्रमाणपत्र सं. / Certificate No.: LD-20250171647

INTELLECTUAL PROPERTY INDIA

सत्यमेव जयते

प्रतिलिप्यधिकार कार्यालय, भारत सरकार | Copyright Office, Government Of India

प्रतिलिप्यधिकार प्रमाणपत्र | Copyright Certificate

प्रतिलिप्यधिकार नियम का नियम 70 | Rule 70 of The Copyright Rules

प्रतिलिप्यधिकार रजिस्टर से उद्धरण | Extracts from the Register of Copyrights

आवेदन सं. / **Application No.:** LD-18062/2025-CO दाखिल करने की तिथि/ **Date of Filing:** 06/05/2025

एतद्द्वारा यह प्रमाणित किया जाता है कि प्रतिलिप्यधिकार अधिनियम, 1957 के प्रावधानों के अनुसार, उपर्युक्त आवेदन में प्रकट किए गए "Study On Sustainability Management: Evaluation of Organizational Sustainability Metrics (A Case On NIKE)" नामक कार्य के लिए प्रतिलिप्यधिकार प्रदान किया गया है।

This is to certify that a copyright has been registered for the work titled "Study On Sustainability Management: Evaluation of Organizational Sustainability Metrics (A Case On NIKE)" as disclosed in the below mentioned application in accordance with the provisions of the Copyright Act,1957.

रचयिता / Authors:

सं. / SNO.	नाम / Name	पता / Address
1	CHITRITA BANERJEE	5/7,P.B.ROAD,BEHALA-700034

स्वामी / Owners:

सं. / SNO.	नाम / Name	पता / Address
1	CHITRITA BANERJEE	5/7,P.B.ROAD,BEHALA-700034

प्रकाशक विवरण / **Publisher Details:**	N.A.
कार्य की भाषा / **Language of the Work:**	English
कार्य का विवरण / **Description of the Work:**	N.A.
(शर्तें / टिप्पणियाँ, यदि कोई हो) / **(Conditions/ Remarks, if any):**	N.A.

आर. ओ. सी. जारी होने की तिथि / **Date of ROC:** 14/08/2025

Registrar of Copyrights

ABOUT THE AUTHOR

Ms. Chitrita Banerjee possesses more than 15 years of experience in Education Management, Consumer Service Management, Retail Management, Teaching and Marketing. She studied Master of Business Administration from Lancaster University Management School, United Kingdom and pursued Executive General Management Program from Indian Institute Of Management (IIM), India. She holds Bachelor's degree in Biotechnology. She has been part of voluntary services with NASSCOM Foundation. Her areas of interest lie in Research Projects, Philanthropic Initiatives and Management Consulting.

PREFACE

The purpose of sustainability management revolves around the approach to integrating economic, social, and governance considerations that lead an organization to achieve its long-term objectives. The essential elements in this case study define the necessity of assessing organizational profitability, ethical labor practices, resource efficiency, and community engagement within an organization.

The presentation of the case study has two sections. The first section explores the organizational sustainability analysis, and the second section offers interactive responses based on the queries that arise from the case. To provide clarity on sustainability management, various models and frameworks are presented in order to assess the current business practices in terms of sustainability and, accordingly, implement future growth strategies that can direct to Net Zero Pathway.

CONTENTS

Case

Teaching Notes

CASE

JUST DO IT! CAN NIKE MAINTAIN A SUSTAINABLE GROWTH STRATEGY AND REMAIN SUSTAINABLE?

Abstract

Nike is a renowned firm in the footwear, apparel, sports equipment, and accessory segments and has seen unparalleled growth over the past two decades. This case reports Nike's growth strategies. Specifically, the analysis suggests that Nike's exceptional growth was, to a large extent, related to its dedicated work on sustainability, particularly focusing on Environmental, Social, and Governance (ESG) criteria.

Learning Objectives

By the end of this case, students will be able to:

- Understand how Nike built a roadmap to sustainable future business performance by Sustainability Strategy Map analysis.
- Assess the current business practices and the possible business strategies for improvement.
- Identifying the strengths and weaknesses of Nike's business by SWOT analysis and sustainability strategy.

Nike Inc.

Nike Inc. is a publicly listed multinational organization that designs, develops and manufactures footwear, apparel, sports equipment and accessories. Nike's retail outlets operate under the brand name Niketown. Founded in 1964 under the Blue Ribbon Sports Inc. brand name, Nike's head office location is near Oregon, United States. Nike's products represent ground-breaking sports innovation, and the brand has considerably impacted communities by structuring creative and diverse global teams. Indeed, Nike has competition and innovation in its DNA, with the brand name Nike taken from the Greek Goddess of Victory.

Innovation is originally the key to Nike's business model and products. Competition and innovation came together and materialized in their first running shoes. Today, Nike is considered to be not only the biggest supplier in the athletic shoes and apparel category but also a major manufacturer of sports equipment. In the 2018 Fortune 500 list, Nike positioned 89th among the largest United States corporations in gross revenue. Nike's iconic brand image is popular for offering products that meet user-centric demands. It can also be considered a major strategic decision to entrench into new business segments.

Nike Business Segments

Nike Inc. functions under three distinct business segments:

- ***NIKE Brand*:** This segment includes various companies under the Nike brand, which are present in multiple regions worldwide, including Asia Pacific, North America, the Greater China Region, Europe, the MENA (Middle East and Africa), and Latin America. Nike's Global Brand Division is also included under Nike Brand.
- ***Converse*:** This segment designs, distributes, licenses, and sells casual sneakers, apparel, and accessories under the trade names Converse, Chuck Taylor, All-Star, One Star, Star Chevron, and Jack Purcell.
- ***Corporate*:** This segment comprises foreign currency hedge gains and losses concerning the revenues yielded by Nike's other operating segments.

Figure 1. Nike Segment Breakdown

[Based On Nike's Q4 FY 2024 ended May 31,2024]

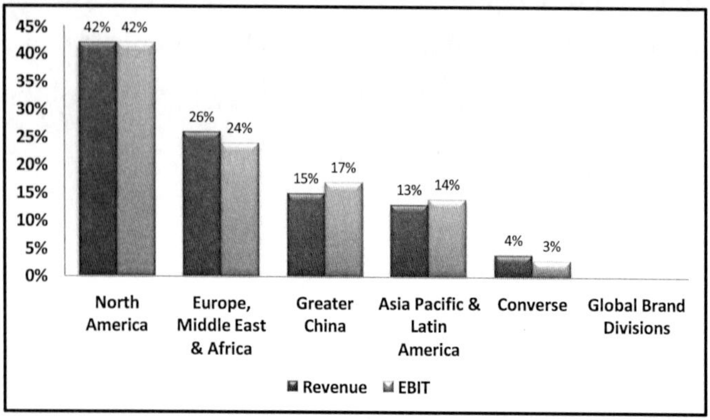

Product Distribution Channels

Nike has three main product distribution channels:

- Nike sells products to wholesalers in the US and foreign markets and is considered the largest distribution network.
- Direct-to-customer (DTC) sales include sales in various forms in retail outlets (in-line or factory outlets) and e-commerce platforms.
- Selling to Global Brand Divisions

Figure 2. Nike's Revenue Worldwide from FY'2016 to FY'2024, by sales channel (in million US Dollars)

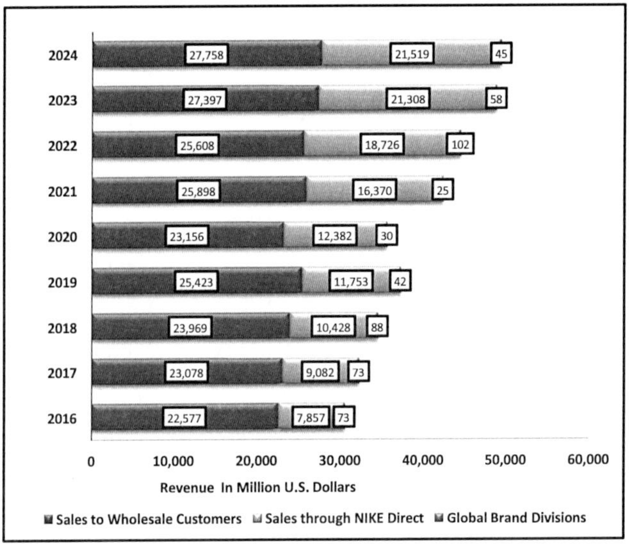

Segmentation and Targeting

Nike's primary consumers are sports enthusiasts. To effectively reach customers, Nike uses four different types of segmentation: demographic, geographic, psychographic, and behavioural segmentation.

Regarding demographic segmentation, Nike targets customers concerning age, gender, occupation, and income status. The brand caters to men, women, and children with high-income backgrounds and within the age group of 15 to 55 years. Geographically, Nike targets customers in urban areas and various international markets. The brand runs different customer-centric promotions tailored to fit diverse lifestyles and cultures. In psychographic segmentation, Nike further targets customers based on personality, lifestyle, activity, interest & preference of customers. Behavioural segmentation allows Nike to analyze customer loyalty and purchase behaviour.

Detailed analysis based on the data collated by market research and by analyzing existing customer base provide valuable insights regarding the target market.

Figure 3. Nike's Market Segmentation Strategy

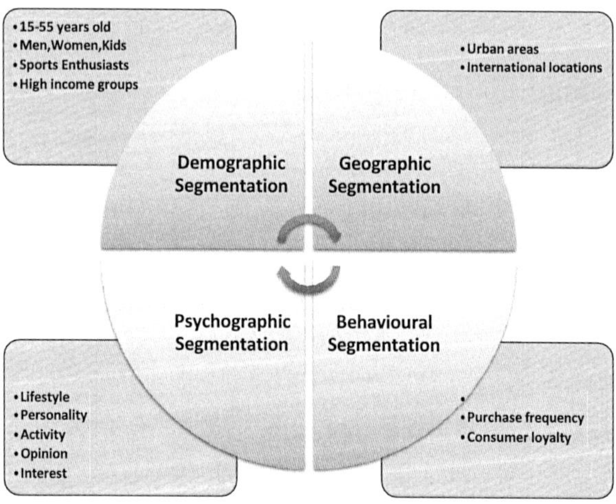

Nike's Financials

Nike has a strong financial record, generating revenue of 51 billion USD in the financial year 2024—an increase of 0.28% in FY'24 compared to FY'23. The change in revenue category-wise has been positive for the NIKE Brand under the category of footwear and equipment, except for apparel. Converse, Corporate Items, and Global brand division have incurred losses post- recovery from the pandemic. The gross profit reflects an increment of nearly 2.6% in the latest financial year.

Income Statement (Figures in thousands, Currency USD)

Column	5/31/2024	5/31/2023	5/31/2022
Total Revenue	51,362,000	51,217,000	46,710,000
Cost Of Revenue	28,475,000	28,925,000	25,231,000
Gross Profit	22,887,000	22,292,000	21,479,000
Operating Expense	16,576,000	16,377,000	14,804,000
Operating Income (EBIT)	6,311,000	5,915,000	6,675,000

NIKE Revenue By Segment (Figures in thousands, Currency USD)

Segment	3/31/2024	3/31/2023	% Change
Footwear	33,740,000	32,570,000	3.59
Equipment	1,930,000	1,680,000	14.88
Apparel	13,690,000	13,850,000	(-)1.15
Converse	2,190,000	2,430,000	(-)9.87
Global Brand Divisions	48,000	92,000	(-)47
Corporate Items	(-)5M	(-)3M	(-)
Total NIKE Brand Revenue	51,362,000	51,217,000	0.28

Nike's assets increased by 1.5% in FY'24. However, total liabilities increased from $23.52 Bn in FY'23 to $23.68 Bn in FY'24. The debt figure in FY'24 amounts to $11.95 Bn. EPS increased by 14.98% in FY'24 compared to FY'23, and the diluted EPS amounts to $3.73 in FY'24.

Balance Sheet (Figures in thousands, Currency USD)

Column	5/31/2024	5/31/2023	5/31/2022
Total Assets	38,110,000	37,531,000	40,321,000
Current Assets	25,382,000	25,202,000	28,213,000
Total non-current Assets	12,728,000	12,329,000	12,108,000
Total Liabilities	23,680,000	23,527,000	25,040,000
Current Liabilities	10,593,000	9,256,000	10,730,000

Column	5/31/2024	5/31/2023	5/31/2022
Total non-current Liabilities	13,087,000	14,271,000	14,310,000
Total Debt	11,952,000	12,144,000	12,627,000

Earning per share	5/31/2024	5/31/2023	% Change
Basic	3.76	3.27	14.98
Diluted	3.73	3.23	15.47

Nike's Sustainability Status

Nike has made considerable efforts to respond to global sustainability challenges. Nike has increasingly emphasized its work on sustainability, stating it as an essential strategic objective aiming to improve the environment and society. Since 2002, Nike has taken action to improve its Environmental, Social, and Governance (ESG) metrics. For example, Nike has consistently focused on reducing its carbon and greenhouse gas footprints. Nike's ESG rating and net impact ratio reflect the present ranking of the organization with respect to the industry competitors based on various sustainability measures, as indicated in Figure 4.

Figure 4. Highlights of Sustainable Developments of Nike

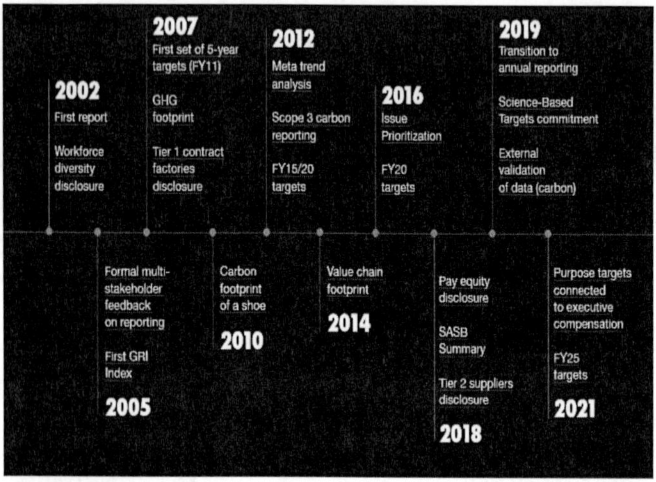

Figure 5. Nike's ESG Rating

Negligible	Low	Medium	High	Severe
0-10	10-20	20-30	30-40	40+

Based on "Sustainalytics" data, Nike's ESG rating of 18.4 denotes that the organization is less hazardous in the textile and apparel sector (Fig. 5). This rating indicates the quantity of industry- specific materials that can cause ESG-related risks and estimates how the organization can tackle the challenges to mitigate the risks.

Approaches to Calculating ESG Rating

Nike's **Exposure-relevant** factors are minimal. The derived exposure score is the quantitative measurement of vulnerability to different materials that can cause ESG issues. Nike's business model reflects the score, including sub-industry and company-specific factors.

While considering **Management-related** factors, Nike scores Average. These factors measure the efficiency of management in handling ESG issues by integrating ESG programs, practices, and policies.

Net Impact Ratio

The mathematical representation of an organization's net impact ratio is equivalent to (total positive impact—total negative impact / total positive impact). The net score is dependent on the variation of different impact categories. The ratio ranges between a minimum value of -∞ and a maximum value of 100%.

Figure 6:Net Impact Ratio

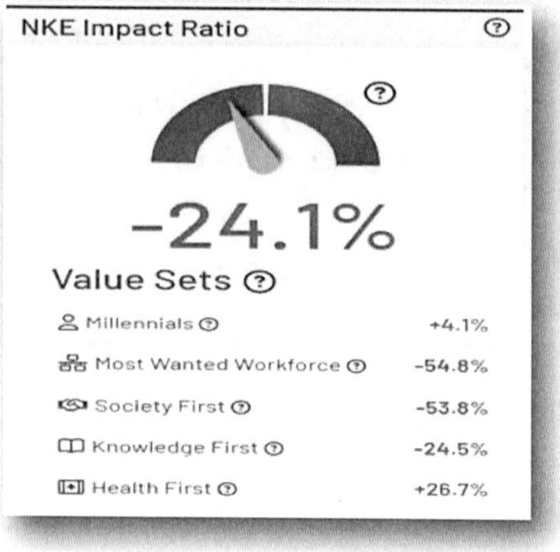

Positive Impact: Nike's most significant positive impact is categorized under the Jobs, Taxes, and Physical Diseases section. The products under the section of Physical Diseases are driven by running shoes, baseball shoes, ski suits, basketball shoes, game equipment, and swimsuits and have maximum positive impact.

Negative Impact: Greenhouse gas (GHG) emissions, waste disposal, and lack of human capital have the maximum negative impact. The main contributing factor has been GHG emissions. Synthetic fibre jackets and coats, synthetic fibre shirts, cotton shorts, synthetic fibre sweaters, cotton shirts, and synthetic fibre sports bra products drive the products under the section of GHG emissions.

Critical Issues in Nike's Business

The accusations against Nike are related to inhuman production practices in developing countries where there are rare instances of enforcing labour laws. There were practices inside Nike's factory where child labour and toxic work culture were encouraged, and factory workers faced appalling working conditions similar to sweatshop factories, where employees had to work long hours with low salaries. Nike even faced allegations regarding gender discrimination. There was a growing need for cultural change within the organization to deal with these issues. This public backlash against Nike arguably has contributed to the current "do good" path operationalized as ESG (Environment, Society & Governance).

Nike has been criticized for using kangaroo leather to manufacture football shoes. This kind of inhuman practice can't be expected from a reputed organization, and the message is clear for Nike that a substitute for kangaroo leather can be the solution.

Sustainability Strategy Map

Implementing innovative, sustainable business strategies can reduce business costs. The sustainability strategy map highlights Nike's present sustainable strategies regarding the Environment, Governance, and Society.

Figure 7. Sustainability Strategic Map Analysis

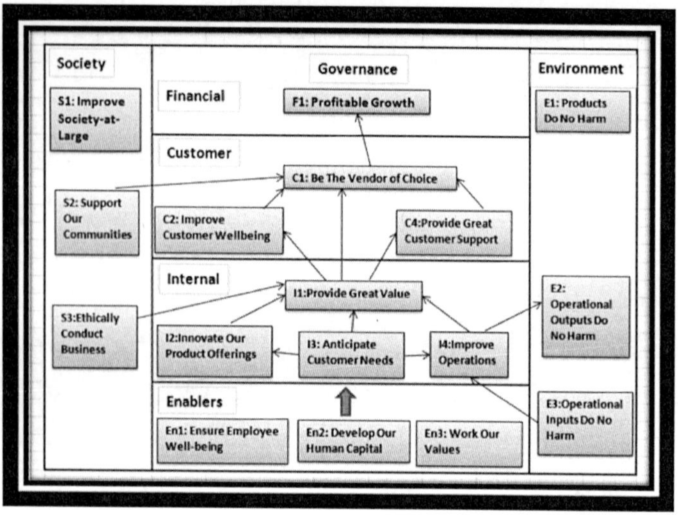

Environment

The organization's environmental impact has been evaluated based on the products that are not harmful to the environment and the operational inputs or outputs that are not environment- friendly.

Products That Do No Harm

The raw materials used to manufacture Nike products are cotton, polyester, rubber, leather and EVA foam. Besides rubber and leather, Nike has increasingly used recycled materials to manufacture its products. In doing so, Nike has successfully reduced 0.5 million metric tonnes of carbon emissions by selecting 50% eco-friendly materials. However, using different forms of rubber and leather can further reduce the carbon footprint in factory outlets. Firstly, to create a new durable product design, Nike can invest in research to develop substitutes for low-impact recycled rubber. Secondly, the generation of high-impact waste and carbon emissions due to leather usage can be minimized by finding alternatives for leather, which can be in the form of synthetic leather or recycled synthetic leather.

Operational Outputs That Do No Harm

The improvement in product design and operational efficiency during the manufacturing and distribution processes, as well as the headquarters management and packaging, have successfully reduced 10% of waste generation per unit. In addition, 100% of waste diversion and 80% of waste reprocessing are streamlined in the supply chain management. The waste from the finished products is usually reused for donations. In terms of water consumption, there has been a reduction in the usage of freshwater by 25% per kg textile for dyeing and finishing. An additional 13 billion litres of water are restored in the supply chain process of cotton.

Nike has worked on the packaging of the products in three different ways that can be considered environmentally sustainable logistics. First, Nike introduced two different-sized boxes by optimizing the design so that the shoes fit within the carton box and all dunnage (plastic and paper) can be channeled into distribution centres to reduce waste. Second, Nike focused on reducing the weight of shipped cartons by 24%. Third, Nike had to look at eliminating plastic for the shoppers visiting retail outlets. However, Nike plans to replace apparel polybags with sustainable, non-plastic alternatives and wants to stop using plastic packaging for digital shipments by introducing paper alternatives.

Operational Inputs That Do No Harm

As Nike aims to achieve Net Zero, consistent efforts to utilize renewable energy or other fuels will be a prerequisite to reduce greenhouse gas emissions from suppliers' manufacturing hubs and delivery-related operations. So far, Nike has achieved the target of reducing greenhouse gas emissions by 70%. The entire process in owned and operated facilities runs on 100% renewable electricity and vehicle electrification. Also, sustainable chemical management practices are encouraged and used for 10 priority chemistries in the entire supply chain

Society

As a profitable organization, Nike has always concentrated on efficient recycling management systems that can reduce waste. However, by assessing social impact, Nike needs to invest in research that can offer solutions for net zero waste and create 100% environment-friendly products.

To uplift society, Nike invested 2% of the previous year's pre-tax income in community development. An additional USD 125 million has been funded to maintain an inclusive community and address racial inequality. Moreover, the organization encourages girls' mandated 50% participation in community building, develops child-responsive urban planning, and sources ecologically sound products.

Governance

Finance: According to the 2021 Federal Income Tax Department data, Nike has accumulated debt for the past three years. The debt figure slightly dropped to USD 11.95 billion in FY'24 compared to FY'23. The outstanding debt has been an area of concern for the organization.

Customer: Customers prefer the Nike brand because the organization prioritizes excellence in product quality and offers innovative designs. Moreover, during the pandemic, Nike launched new region-specific service centres to handle customer complaints.

Internal: The Nike brand is trusted by consumers because it consistently maintains standardized, reliable products. Furthermore, integrating advanced technologies (AI, blockchain, and robots) in the supply chain has increased the efficiency of operations manifold. To support circular supply chain, Nike uses different types of freight methods to minimize carbon emissions.

Enablers: To promote diversity in the workplace, Nike has a fixed target FY'25 and plans to maintain the ratio of participation of certain segments of the population in specific roles:

(1) 50 % of women representation in the corporate workplace and 45% women representation in leadership roles (2) In the role of Director and above, 30% representation of US racial and ethnic minorities (3) In the US corporate workforce, 35% representation of US racial and ethnic minorities.

In addition to these measures, Nike plans to invest USD10 million in Colleges and Universities for Black communities and Hispanic-serving institutions. The funding was also doubled for the career progression of racial and ethnic minorities in the US and women internationally.

Concerning the suppliers, USD1 billion was invested in maintaining diverse suppliers. The strategic suppliers successfully measure or improve worker engagement, building a safe and healthy workplace. Nike ensures that the suppliers maintain health and safety protocols. Additionally, there has been no discrimination among employees of different genders concerning annual payscale at any hierarchical level.

Nike implements recruitment marketing strategies to hire and attract first-line athletes who can compete for corporate roles. Nike's mission is to provide access for athletes with disabilities. As an organization that supports engagement and inclusivity, Nike ranks among the leading organizations. Nike's employee engagement program related to inclusive leadership ensures that the current employees working as vice presidents participate in the program.

Key Partners

Nike maintains relationships with various global partners that include governing bodies, and organizations to enhance manufacturing efficiency. This collaboration offers sustainable, innovative products that meet customer needs and environmental challenges. The key collaborations of Nike to manage the supply chain can throw light on which variety of supplier partnerships are given priority while structuring the present business strategy. Supplier alliances can enhance operational efficiency and can be a measure of sustainable business solutions. Nike has worked on developing relationships with partners who can help supply manufactured products, improve facility management, strengthen local laws, maintain diversity and inclusion in the workplace, offer sustainable solutions, and improve supply chain management. As such, these partnerships demonstrate a capability to nurture its ESG strategy.

Supplier Partnerships

Since its inception, Nike has carefully developed five meaningful partnerships with suppliers. Pou Chen Corporation, considered the largest manufacturer in the branded athletic and casual footwear sector in the world, manufactures products for Nike. Since its foundation in Taiwan, the manufacturer has established factories in China, Indonesia, Vietnam, Bangladesh, Cambodia, and Myanmar. The other Taiwan-based manufacturer, Fulgent Sun Group, produces shoes in Vietnam, Cambodia, and China.

The third supplier partnership is with PT Pan Brothers, which has a presence throughout Indonesia. The supplier manufactures Nike's apparel products, such as fall and winter jackets, pants, shorts, casual pants, dress shirts, snowboarding and ski outwear, polo shirts, golf shirts, tracksuits, sweatsuits, and other activewear.

The fourth supplier partnership is with Delta Galil Industries, an Israeli-based private-label apparel company. They manufacture intimate apparel, socks, and activewear for Nike and have factories throughout Southeast Asia.

The fifth is the Hong Kong-based Eagle Nice International Holdings, which has manufacturing facilities in China, Vietnam, and Indonesia. It manufactures down jackets, sweaters, sports pants, and other sportswear for Nike.

Partnerships for Sustainable Business Solutions

Nike has nurtured various alliances for sustainability. Nike achieved agendas related to maintaining agricultural standards, improving labour conditions, and promoting gender diversity within the organization. The key stakeholders who played an instrumental role in identifying the requisite tools and approaches to strengthen human rights and solve sustainability challenges include government, business, trade unions, civil society, and institutions.

Nike's agreement with the Social Labor Convergence Program (SLCP) and members of the Sustainable Apparel Coalition has ensured consistent and sustainable performance with the business partners. Moreover, by substituting audit-related tools, SLCP helps gauge labour, health, and safety conditions while working in factories. In addition, Nike conducts programs with the Fair Labor Association to improve employee functions in the factories.

Nike has a collaboration platform called Sustainable Apparel Coalition, which includes over 200 leading apparel, footwear, retailers, suppliers, and academic institutions. The online assessment tools offered by The Coalition (Higg Index suite) standardize the measurement of the ecological impacts of apparel and footwear products. Nike uses the Higg Facility Environment module to analyze data collated from suppliers responsible for finished goods and determines environmental performance impact within the organization.

To maintain sustainability while manufacturing the raw materials of Nike products, Nike has taken initiatives by jointly working with Better Cotton Initiative (BCI), NGO Textile Exchange, Leather Working group, NGO Ceres and NGO BSR. These associations help farmers limit the usage of water, chemical pesticides, and fertilizers and ensure responsible expansion of textiles across the global textile value chain. They assist in combatting environmental challenges, protecting water utilization, reducing pollution, and controlling human rights violations to build an inclusive economy, leading to improved yields, profitability, and livelihood. In addition, Nike has associated with BCI to maintain Nike's conventional cotton balance in terms of BCI standards and has added value to the farmers. Sustainable Business Network (BSR) has worked closely with Nike to implement sustainable business solutions through consulting, research and cross-sector collaborations.

Certain associations of Nike are goal-driven, and the purpose is to achieve the organizational climate targets by 2050. One of these associations is the Fashion Industry Charter for Climate Action (the United Nations Climate Change) where Nike can work with the suppliers to reduce green house gas emissions. Likewise, the Arctic Shipping Pledge directs Nike to minimize commitments of shipments during international freight transfers.

Partnerships to Maintain Diversity and Inclusion

In maintaining diversity and inclusion, Nike has worked mainly on training communities and supporting girls and young members in sports. The tie-up with Peace Players International promotes sports among youth leaders by forming communities. Nike, along with the organization Mentor, offers a program to eliminate the 'mentoring gap' among the young generation so that they receive the relevant support necessary to succeed in life. The network of local NGO Girls Inc., operating from the United States and Canada, has joined hands with Nike to serve girls (aged 6-18 years) in building a foundation in the field of sports, adventure, and physical activity throughout their lives under the Program "Sporting Chance".

Discussion Questions

1. Conduct a SWOT analysis of Nike. What are the main threats and opportunities for the business? What role does sustainability play in future growth?
2. Considering Miles and Snow's framework, which organization category does Nike best match? How may sustainability alter Miles and Snow's Framework? Support your arguments with evidence from the case.
3. Critically examine Nike's current Sustainability Strategy Map: What are the key weaknesses concerning its value chain configuration? How can Nike better align the value chain and their Sustainability Strategy Map?

TEACHING NOTES

JUST DO IT! CAN NIKE MAINTAIN A SUSTAINABLE GROWTH STRATEGY AND REMAIN SUSTAINABLE?

Case Summary

This case illustrates a holistic view of Nike's business model with a particular emphasis on sustainability. In hindsight, a balanced approach of the development of Nike's strategic supplier relationship to meet the potential market demand has been elaborated. Moreover, the case simultaneously analyzes Nike's recent and past developmental measures supporting their sustainability initiatives and has an essential role in augmenting their business performance. The case provides qualitative, soft-side measures and more quantitative or hard-side measures to help students better grasp Nike's sustainability initiatives and their effects. To this end, the case provides readers with i) some important sources and measures to assess a firm's sustainability strategy and ii) comprehensive material for discussions centred around sources of sustainability- oriented strategy development to achieve business growth. The case, therefore, provides some clues to developing a growth strategy for a net zero sustainable pathway.

Teaching Objectives

Nike case offers some perspectives on sustainability to students who study business models, sustainable operations management, and strategic analysis (including formulation and implementation), to name a few. More specifically, students will be able to enhance their understanding of the following:

- Parameters that can affect a brand's identity and the scope of improvement for sustainable development
- Factors determining the sustainability status of consumer goods companies
- The importance of different types of partnerships for sustainable business strategies
- How to use economic, social and governance (ESG) measures for developing sustainable business models and strategies

Target Audience

This case study is intended for postgraduate-level students, including, but not limited to, BSc, MSc, MBA, and Executive MBA students. It suits students studying basic to intermediate levels of sustainable business model innovation, strategic management, strategic leadership, sustainable strategy, strategic change, and strategy development.

Suggested Teaching Strategy

While strategic management courses are taught in many different ways and include a variety of lenses, such as behavioural views, cognitive views, practice lenses, process views, and competitive strategy, this case has taken a pragmatic perspective. The differing opinions allow some degree of flexibility in teachers' intended area and style of use. However, we envisage at least two ways to use the case.

The first approach is to use the case as a group exercise. Teachers could ask students integrating questions that prompt them to link different parts of Nike's sustainability strategy to make sense of its complexity. Such an exercise suits students taking intermediate-level strategy courses or courses that build on some basic understanding of strategy or sustainability concepts.

The second approach to using this case is for classroom or seminar discussion exercises. The teacher could use the entire case as a basis for discussion or divide it into segments for reflection and discussion among groups of students. Such an approach could use the guiding questions at the end of the case as starting points and expand beyond them. Still, teachers may develop other discussion topics or questions to prompt students to seek relevant information and get involved in critical reflection individually and in groups. In either scenario, teachers, teaching assistants, or designated students are expected to moderate discussions.

Our suggestion is to prompt students to search for additional data and information; it entirely depends on whichever approach is adopted. The critical analysis approach will help students see potential changes in Nike's sustainability strategy and update their analysis accordingly. The suggested solutions to discussion questions (found below) are primarily based on information found in the case and complemented with some additional information collated from different authentic resources.

Suggested Solutions for Discussion Questions

1) ***Conduct a SWOT analysis of Nike. What are the main threats and opportunities for the business?***

   What role does sustainability play in future growth? A detailed observation and introspection of the varied departments of the organization can reveal the potential factors responsible for business growth and the scope of improvement. There will be further data-driven, fact-based analysis that can determine the pitfalls, and the organization needs to pay special attention. Finally, the discussion delves into what prospects Nike can plan for future market expansion.

Strengths

- The Nike brand is highly recognized for its product quality, durability, and association with fitness. Nike is the preferred brand for athletes and youth.
- The brand has always conducted research to continuously improve every product, resulting in several innovations and brand recognition.
- Nike has the highest market share in the athletic apparel, accessories, and footwear sectors.
- The powerful brand identity of Nike has assisted in developing a successful brand presence internationally.
- The brand has several celebrity athlete endorsements, including Michael Jordon, Bo Jackson, Ronaldinho,

Wayne Rooney, Kobe Bryant, Roger Federer, Rafael Nadal, Lebron James, Cristiano Ronaldo, Colin Kaepernick, and Serena Williams.

- Nike's campaigns and advertisements attract customers' sentiments. The advertisements can connect with customers with a compelling message. The storytelling engagement can be related to the ad campaign 'For Once, Don't Do It,' which aims to support the Black community against racism.

Weaknesses

- In certain foreign countries, Nike's labour conditions need special attention. Several issues that do not abide by labour laws include forced labour, child labour, low wages, and substandard working conditions (regarded as insecure for workers). The impact on the brand image is relatively high due to the poor working conditions in overseas manufacturing hubs.
- Though Nike has a promising growth story, it has incurred a debt of $11.95 billion in the current financial year 2024.
- Even though Nike has a worldwide presence, it depends heavily on the US market, with a high share of sales concentrated in the US. According to the revenue report 2024, the revenue generated from the US market contributed to approximately 43% of the total

revenue, and Nike's remaining income was generated from other regional markets.

Figure 1. Nike Revenue Worldwide from FY'2017 to FY'2024, by region (in million US Dollars)

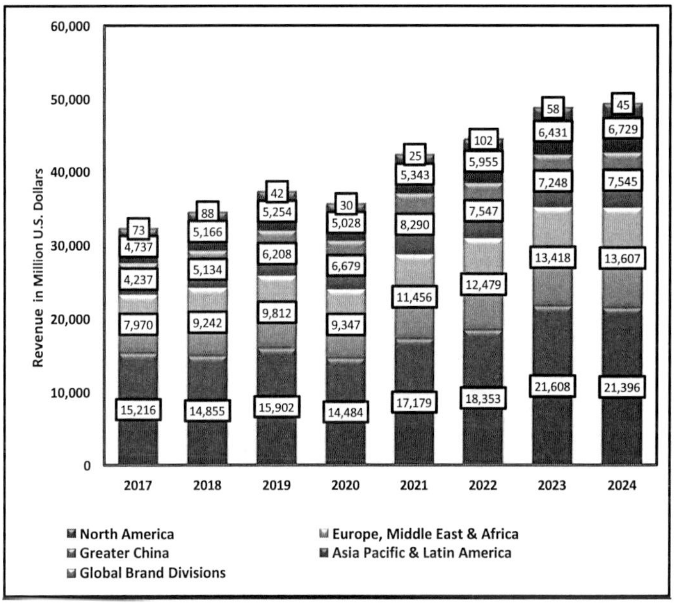

- Nike faced legal allegations from female employees regarding the workplace culture. The major concerns raised included unsafe environment for women, instances of sexual misconduct and gender-biased practices with respect to payscale and career progression. These lawsuits can serve as negative criticism and can degrade the brand's reputation.

- While the footwear business remains the largest product category, contributing nearly 68% of revenue, this data underscores the need for diversification. Moreover, Nike must build the capability to diversify by developing new categories or adding new products to its present categories.

Figure 2. Revenue Share of Nike Worldwide in FY'24 by Product Category

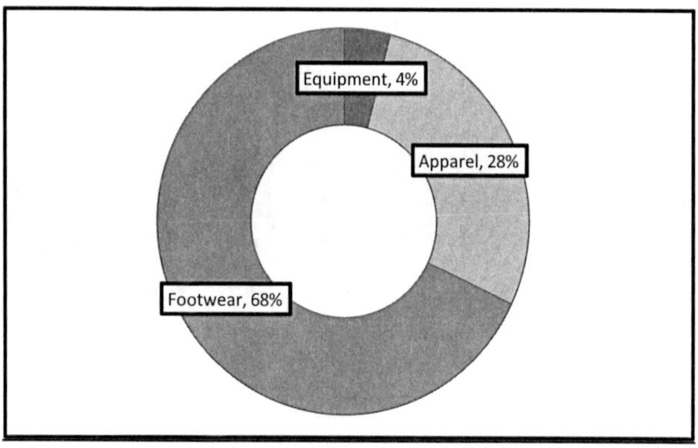

Opportunities

- Nike has gained a foothold in several foreign countries. This success paves the way for further expansion in various emerging markets such as India, Brazil, and China. This international market diversification will be a promising opportunity for future growth.

- Innovative products that combine technology will produce tech-savvy utility-specific items. For instance, advanced athletic wear is manufactured using modern technology and can also be considered a fashion statement for consumers.
- Since the pandemic, consumer preferences related to shopping behaviour have shifted from brick-and-mortar purchases to e-retail shopping. Therefore, the digital shopping experience for consumers can be the best means to attract customers. An increased budget allocation for digital marketing expenditures can ensure Nike's effort is channeled for a better e-retail consumer experience and can increase sales revenue.
- The acquisition of Artificial Intelligence organizations or start-ups offering data-driven business solutions with a measure of inventory predictability can improve online sales capabilities and customer shopping experience.
- To embrace next-generation collectables, Nike acquired RTFKT, a brand capable of merging culture and gaming. This association will help develop different kinds of virtual products and experiences by implementing the latest technologies of game engines, NFTs (non-fungible tokens), blockchain authentication, and artificial simulation.

- Nike works with a start-up, Grabit, which can speed up the manufacturing process by using advanced assembly machines.

Threats

- The competitive market and the arrival of new brands are possible threats to Nike. Hence, the brand must maintain uniqueness in products and services to compete.
- Volatile foreign exchange rates can impact Nike's global operations because operational expenses vary greatly. Concurrently, financial earnings in US dollars vary based on the valuation of other foreign currencies.
- Adidas' patent-related disputes against Nike can impact the brand's reputation. Negative word of mouth regarding legal disputes can tarnish Nike's brand image.
- Nike faced lawsuits on intellectual property rights from the Skechers brand. In response, Nike proved that Sketchers made duplicates of Nike's Air Max 270 and VaporMax product designs. It is imperative for Nike to maintain every legal evidence pertaining to the respective products so that during emergencies, immediate legal actions can be taken against the competitors.
- The investigation against Nike reveals that the organization used kangaroo skin to manufacture

leather football shoes. This fact has given rise to the impression that the organization works on principles based only on profitability and does not value animal protection.

- Different retailers and merchandisers sell low-quality counterfeit Nike products at cheaper prices, which attract customers. Implementing strategic decisions to separate counterfeit products from the original brand can ensure that customers can distinctly verify Nike as a brand by checking the packaging, unique logo design, or hallmark.
- Trade tensions caused by geopolitical events in different parts of the globe can cause labour strikes. It is difficult for the organization to control the global supply chain. These situations can profoundly impact the business, and as a brand, effective countermeasures to tackle trade tensions are necessary.

2) ***Considering Miles and Snow's framework, which category of organization does Nike best match? How may sustainability alter Miles and Snow's Framework? Support your arguments with evidence from the case.***

The assessment of organizational problems related to entrepreneurial (managing market share), operational (implementing solutions to address entrepreneurial issues), and administrative (managing entrepreneurial and operational issues) can help understand what kind of business solutions are required to overcome the challenges. The insights revealed what strategies can help expand the existing business and the approach to launch new products or enter a new market.

Market Penetration: This strategy is implemented when the organization is confident of increasing product sales because of the strong existing business connections.

- Due to the growing population in the emerging Asian markets, Nike can increase sales due to higher demand, allowing it to capture additional market share.
- Offering competitive pricing to customers by lowering overhead costs location-wise can appeal to customers in the respective market. Product quality and price can be the main determinants of high sales volume.
- Customer needs and shopping patterns vary in different markets. Hence, communication channels have to advertise products that suit consumer needs. Advertisements can be the best way to draw customers' attention in various locations.
- Nike has been slowly progressing towards adapting the e-commerce shopping experience and concentrating on improving capabilities for social commerce (developing shopping- centric apps for customer engagement and help in conversion to sales), "Sneakerheads Platform" ('SNRKS" app that creates demand for

shoes targeted towards most-engaged customers) and Analytics (understanding consumer preferences and designing new products by collecting data using a digital ecosystem). However, based on the market, campaign and content management strategies must be customized to draw the attention of the relevant target audience within the same market.

Nike has a strong base in the US and recently developed strategic distributor partnerships in Brazil, Chile, Argentina, and Uruguay. Nike must target similar strategic alliances in other emerging countries to expand its business.

Market Development: Market development strategy involves leveraging and selling existing products to different markets.

- Nike can invest in research and development in different markets to understand customers' culture, consumer behaviour and market trends. This variation will help identify possible market and customer segments.
- When Nike focuses on regional expansion, cultural differences have to be considered, and accordingly, Nike products can be customized based on market needs.
- Nike can target different customer segments in the same market for existing products. In addition,

increased visibility by various modes of marketing can improve brand recall and augment sales.

- There is a need to educate consumers regarding Nike products in new markets. The various engagement activities of Nike can allow consumers to understand product features related to usage and how the product differentiates from competitors.

Product Development: Investing in research and development for innovation can help develop a new product or add new features to existing products, which can target the existing customer base.

- Understanding the new product development process by identifying changing customer needs and investing in research and development to modify existing products or launch a new product. Nike can think of launching products that can be considered next-generation trendsetters, such as smart clothing that can monitor body conditions during exercise and detect health-related abnormalities.
- In order to remain competitive in the market, Nike needs to consistently invest in research and development to showcase creativity and introduce innovations.
- Strategic partnerships will help develop new products and assess their development process or market acceptability.

Diversification: Diversification is the highest-risk strategy involving both product and market development. There are two possible types of diversification–related diversification (potential merger between existing business and new product or market) and unrelated diversification (unrelated industry mergers between existing business and new product or market). These types of diversification may take place differently at Nike:

- Vertical diversification by new product development and launches under existing product groups and categories of Nike
- Horizontal diversification is achieved through new product development and launches that are not associated with Nike's product groups or categories.
- Through mergers and acquisitions, Nike can diversify into different businesses and explore conglomerate growth to create entirely new businesses. For example, by acquiring other organizations, Nike can focus on diversifying into the gaming or fitness industries.
- Nike can enter new markets or target new consumer segments by offering entirely new products unrelated to existing ones.

In-depth research on Nike's market penetration, market development, product development, and diversification highlights its current functioning and the scope for improvement in exploiting new products and market opportunities. In a fast-changing business environment, Nike has always prioritized promoting creativity to meet evolving consumer demands. However, refining the administration process is also necessary to ensure the smooth execution of diverse, sustainable business activities and maintain its position as a market leader.

3) *Critically examine Nike's current Sustainability Strategy Map: What are the key weaknesses concerning its value chain configuration? How can Nike better align the value chain and their Sustainability Strategy Map?*

Implementing innovative, sustainable business strategies can reduce business costs. The sustainability strategy map can highlight Nike's present sustainable strategies with respect to the Environment, Society, and Governance and the areas that need improvement.

Environment Factors

Products Do No Harm:

- Nike has successfully reduced 0.5 million metric tonnes of carbon emissions by using 50% environmentally preferred materials.

Operational Outputs Do No Harm:

- Nike has reduced waste per unit by 10% in manufacturing, distribution, headquarters, and packaging by improving design and operational efficiency.
- Nike diverted 100% of waste and recycled 80% of waste in manufacturing, packaging, distribution centres and headquarters
- 10 times of finished goods waste have been recycled or used for donation
- Nike reduced freshwater usage for dyeing and finishing by 25% per kg textile.
- Restoration of water of 13 billion litres in the supply chain process of cotton

Packaging Highlights:

I. Introduced two new sizes of boxes to improve the fit of the shoes within the carton box and phased out all dunnage (both plastic and paper) in distribution centres, reducing waste.

II. Reduced weight of shipping cartons by 24%.

III. Eliminated plastic shoppers in all retail centres. However, Nike is working on replacing apparel polybags with more sustainable, non-plastic alternatives and plans to eliminate plastic packaging for digital shipments with a paper alternative.

Operational Inputs Do No Harm

- Achieved a 70% reduction in greenhouse gas emissions in owned and operated facilities using 100% renewable electricity and fleet electrification.
- As Nike targets Net Zero, consistent efforts to utilize renewable energy or other fuels will be a prerequisite to reducing greenhouse gas emissions from suppliers' manufacturing hubs and delivery-related operations.
- Sustainable chemical management practices are encouraged for 10 priority chemistries in the supply chain. The company Bluesign Technologies works with Nike as partner to provide assessment tools for bluesign technology. By using these tools, suppliers can have access to different types of dyes, detergents, and chemicals that are useful for manufacturing sustainable textile materials.

Societal Factors

Improve Society at Large: Nike invested 2% of the previous year's pre-tax income in community development to uplift society.

Support Communities

- Nike invested an additional USD 125 million to maintain an inclusive community and address racial inequality.

- The organization encourages girls' mandatory 50% participation in community building, develops child-responsive urban planning, and sources environmentally friendly products.
- Nike, along with the Nike Foundation, allocated fund of $30million for humanitarian activities during Covid-19. During this time of crisis, Nike also received support from the WHO (World Health Organisation) and various other local NGOs based out around the world. Moreover, Nike partnered with the World Federation of the Sporting Goods Industry (WFSGI) to endorse campaigns organized by WHO related to physical fitness.

Ethically Conduct Business

As a profitable organization, Nike has always concentrated on efficient recycling management systems that can reduce waste. However, by assessing social impact, Nike needs to invest in research that can offer solutions for net zero waste and create 100% environment-friendly products.

Governance Factors

Finance: According to the 2021 Federal Income Tax Department data, Nike has accumulated debt for three years. The debt figure dropped slightly to USD 11.95 billion in FY'24 compared to FY'23. The accumulated liabilities have been a significant area of concern for the organization.

Customers: Nike has successfully attracted customers' attention by maintaining its brand image and product quality and continuously innovating new product designs. Moreover, during COVID-19, Nike opened new service centres to address customer grievances better and ensure quick delivery without failure.

Internal: Nike has created a brand identity that always showcases high-value products. Furthermore, incorporating AI, blockchain, and robots in the supply chain has ensured the seamless execution of operations. Nike overcame the challenges of shortage of staffs during the pandemic by implementing robots and ensuring that the robots execute labour-related tasks during order processing. For domestic transportation of goods in the US, Nike only ships products via land.

Enablers

- Ensured representation of 50 % of women in the corporate workplace and 45% in leadership roles.
- 30% of US racial and ethnic minorities are represented in the director roles and above.
- In the US corporate workforce, there has been a representation of 35% of US racial and ethnic minorities.

- Nike invested an additional $10 million in institutions built for Black Colleges and Universities and Hispanic societies.
- Doubling investment for professional development of racial and ethnic minorities in the US and women globally.
- Nike utilized an investment of $1 billion to maintain diverse suppliers.
    1. 100% strategic suppliers assist in building a workplace that is safe and healthy.
    2. Additionally, strategic suppliers have been successful in measuring and improving worker engagement.
    3. Improved health and safety protocols for suppliers.
    4. Ensured 100% equal pay opportunity annually for all employees at every hierarchical level.
    5. Provide opportunities and marketing of open roles for first-line athletes so that they can compete for corporate roles.
    6. Nike stands in the top quartile of benchmarked companies with a strong focus on engagement and inclusion.
    7. 100% of Vice Presidents completed the Inclusive Leadership Program.

Application Of Value Chain Analysis to Identify Weaknesses

Primary Activities directly affect the production of the product or execution of the service. Specific attention is needed in the production process related to inbound logistics, operations, and outbound logistics.

Inbound Logistics

Nike uses superior-quality raw materials to manufacture high-quality finished goods. However, Nike can save production costs by reducing damage during product transfer.

Operations

The availability of cheap labour in emerging country manufacturing hubs has been the primary strategy behind Nike's increase in the profit margin of its products. However, Nike needs to constantly revise its HR practices and salary thresholds to avoid issues related to forced labour, gender pay gaps and local minimum laws and regulation violations.

Sales and Marketing

Nike can increase online sales by digitally reaching out to the right audience. Nike needs to monitor consumer reviews for every product on the company website and third-party e- commerce sites. Various kinds of promotions can be targeted for customers on the online platform.

Secondary activities affect the primary activities, giving Nike a competitive advantage by improving efficiency. Nike must focus on sustainable procurement options to materialize this synchronization of activities.

Procurement

Nike manufactures products by procuring six varieties of raw materials: Polyester, Rubber, EVA Foam, Cotton, Synthetic leather, and Leather. To uphold its sustainability agenda, Nike constantly revises and updates conditions for raw materials in its products to ensure that the standards meet local and most recent environmental laws and regulations and broader public expectations.

Aligning value chain and sustainability strategy after consolidated research findings on Nike regarding the current sustainability strategy status and understanding the weaknesses by analyzing the Value Chain, it is possible to find out what possible business solutions Nike can invest in that can lead to the organization's sustainability.

Nike's sales on digital platforms increased year over year. Therefore, Nike needs to stay alert to potential disruptive forces that could change this positive trend and ensure that its investments in digital advertisements augment online sales.

Nike's next big challenge is reliance on the US market to generate revenue. Nike can focus on growing business in developing nations like China and India because of its high population density. In addition, there has been an increased dependency on Nike's footwear sales, and the organization can diversify into unrelated businesses in the wellness and gaming industries. Therefore, investing in market research in new markets can lead to a regional understanding of consumer behaviours. Market research can also be a tool to estimate whether the customers prefer any new product. Nike can further enhance customer experience by utilizing artificial intelligence (AI) technologies, and it is requisite that Nike look into the acquisition of AI start-ups. Moreover, while devising strategies in new markets, Nike can form alliances with companies with strong networks in different countries.

The consolidated research on Nike concerning sustainable development highlights that though Nike has made considerable progress that can direct the organization towards the Net Zero goal, investment in research and development can still provide solutions (related to using raw materials or manufacturing the products) that are completely environment friendly.

Using animal skin to manufacture specific products by well-known Nike can associate the brand not in support of protecting animals. An immediate action from the organization will be to find a substitute for animal skin, and by doing so, Nike can restore the brand's reputation. In addition, workplace-related issues such as gender discrimination, child labour, and toxic work culture for women need to be handled by implementing policies and monitoring the organizational culture. Sometimes, the organization might have to change its culture to deal with these issues.

The future of Nike is dependent on the profitability of the business along with its efficiency, which will lead to the Net Zero pathway. The strategic decisions directed towards selecting environmentally preferred materials, utilizing renewable energy in factories, and working across industries can be the determinants to accelerate progress.

REFERENCES

Alan, B. & Emma, B. (2011) *Business Research Methods.* Oxford: Oxford University Press.

Blake, B. (2022) Adidas sues Nike over run-tracking, shoe-adjusting technologies. *Reuters,* 11 June. Available at: https://www.reuters.com/legal/litigation/adidas-sues-nike-over-run-tracking-shoe-adjusting-technologies-2022-06-10/#:~:text=The%20lawsuit%20filed%20in%20East,%22%20system%2C%20and%20other%20technology. [Accessed 23 April 2025].

Bloomberg (2017) These Robots Are Using Static Electricity to Make Nike Sneakers. *Fortune,* 30 August. Available at: https://fortune.com/2017/08/30/robots-static-electricity-nike-sneakers/ [Accessed 23 April 2025].

Cara, S. (2019) 'Behind closed doors': The friction between the Nike brand and its corporate culture. *Retail Dive,* 3 September. Available at: https://www.retaildive.com/news/behind-closed-doors-the-friction-between-the-nike-brand-and-its-corporat/561608/ [Accessed 23 April 2025].

Cascale (n.d.) *We Are Cascale.* Available at: https://cascale.org [Accessed 23 April 2025].

CIO Wiki (2022) Miles and Snow's Organizational Strategies. 29 November. Available at: https://cio-wiki.org/wiki/Miles_and_Snow%27s_Organizational_Strategies [Accessed 27 April 2025].

CIPS. (2023) How Nike transformed supply chains to survive Covid. 24 October. Available at: https://www.cips.org/supply-management/news/2022/january/how-nike-transformed-supply-chains-to-survive-covid/ [Accessed 23 April 2025].

Dani, J. (2022) Adidas sues Nike for alleged patent infringement, targets mobile applications. *Retail Dive,*15 June. Available at: https://www.retaildive.com/news/adidas-sues-nike-patent-infringement-mobile-apps/625513/ [Accessed 23 April 2025].

Edward, H. (2018) Nike hit with lawsuit from four women who allege gender discrimination. *Business & Human Rights Resource Centre,* 10 August. Available at: https://www.business-humanrights.org/en/latest-news/nike-hit-with-lawsuit-from-four-women-who-allege-gender-discrimination/ [Accessed 23 April 2025].

Eric (2016) Is Nike the Next Big Tech Giant?. *Harvard Business School Digital Initiative*, 18 November. Available at: https://digital.hbs.edu/platform-rctom/submission/is-nike-the-next-big- tech-giant/ [Accessed 23 April 2025].

Kurt, B. (2016) Why Cristiano Ronaldo's $1 Billion Nike Deal May Be A Bargain For Sportswear Giant. *Forbes*, 2 December. Available at: https://www.forbes.com/sites/kurtbadenhausen/2016/12/02/cristiano-ronaldos-1-billion-nike-deal-is-a-bargain-for-sportswear-giant/ [Accessed 23 April 2025].

Investopedia (2022) Nike Stock: Analyzing 5 Key Suppliers (NKE).23 December. Available at: https://www.investopedia.com/articles/markets/051416/nike-stock-analyzing-5-key-suppliers-nke.asp [Accessed 23 April 2025].

Jemima, W.(2021) Nike Accused Of Driving Kangaroos To Extinction To Make Leather Football Shoes. *Plant Based News,*

20 December. Available at: https://plantbasednews.org/culture/ethics/nike-kangaroos-leather-football-shoes/ [Accessed 23 April 2025].

Jessica,G.(2018) Nike accused of fostering hostile workplace in new gender discrimination lawsuit. *CNBC Online,*10 Aug. Available at: https://www.cnbc.com/2018/08/10/ex-nike-employees-sue-over-gender-discrimination-hostile-workplace.html?msockid=223929dd27d864440dc33c1226b0653b [Accessed 23 April 2025].

Kyle, P. (2025) Ansoff Matrix. *Corporate Finance Institute.* Available at: https://corporatefinanceinstitute.com/resources/knowledge/strategy/ansoff-matrix/ [Accessed 23 April 2025].

Lawrence, G. (2024) Nike's Marketing Mix (4P) Analysis. *Panmore Institute,* 13 August. Available at: https://panmore.com/nike-inc-marketing-mix-4ps-product-place-promotion-price-analysis [Accessed 23 April 2025].

Marketbeat (2025) Nike (NKE) ESG Score & Sustainability Data. 5 February. Available at: https://www.marketbeat.com/stocks/NYSE/NKE/sustainability/ [Accessed 23 April 2025].

Matthew, J. (2024) How Nike Makes Money. *Investopedia,* 10 June. Available at: https://www.investopedia.com/articles/markets/080415/how-nike-nke-makes-its-money.asp [Accessed 23 April 2025].

Mohit, O. (2020) Analyzing Nike's Distribution Channels and Retail Strategy. *Market Realist,* 25 July. Available at:: https://marketrealist.com/2019/10/analyzing-nikes-distribution-channels-and-retail-strategy/#:~:text=1%20Selling%20products%20to%20wholesalers%20in%20the%20US,Nike%20Direct%20is%20the%20company's%20fastest-growing%20distribution%20channel. [Accessed 23 April 2025].

Upright Project (2024) *Net Impact*. Available at: https://docs.uprightplatform.com/metrics//net-impact [Accessed 23 April 2025].

Nike (2024) *FY23 NIKE, Inc. Impact Report.*[pdf]Available at: https://about.nike.com/en/newsroom/releases/fy23-nike-inc-impact-report [Accessed 23 April 2025].

Nike (2020) *NIKE, INC. ANNOUNCES STRATEGIC DISTRIBUTOR PARTNERSHIPS IN BRAZIL, ARGENTINA, CHILE AND URUGUAY.* Available at:

https://investors.nike.com/investors/news-events-and-reports/investor-news/investor-news-details/2020/NIKE-Inc-Announces-Strategic-Distributor-Partnerships-In-Brazil-Argentina-Chile- and-Uruguay/default.aspx [Accessed 23 April 2025].

Nike (n.d.) *What is Nike's Mission?*. Available at: https://www.nike.com/help/a/nikeinc-mission?msockid=1987a772c88e6bee33f1b2a6c9676a32 [Accessed 23 April 2025].

Nike (n.d.) *Sustainable Development Goals (SDGs).* Available at: https://about.nike.com/en/impact-resources/sustainable-development-goals-sdgs [Accessed 23 April 2025].

Nike (n.d.) *Moving Forward Together.* Available at: https://about.nike.com/en/impact [Accessed 23 April 2025].

Nike (n.d.) *Impact Partnerships and Collaborations.* Available at: https://purpose.nike.com/partnerships-collaborations [Accessed 23 April 2025].

Nike (2021) *Nike Acquires RTFKT.* Available at: https://about.nike.com/en/newsroom/releases/nike-acquires-rtfkt [Accessed 23 April 2025].

Nike (2021) *COVID-19 Response Effort.* Available at: https://about.nike.com/en/impact-resources/covid-19-response-efforts [Accessed 23 April 2025].

Nike (2005) *Impact Partnerships and Collaborations.* Available at:https://about.nike.com/en/impact-resources/impact-partnerships-and-collaborations [Accessed 23 April 2025].

Nike (n.d.) *How Can I Get Nike's Best Deals?.*Available at: https://www.nike.com/help/a/product-discount [Accessed 23 April 2025].

Nike (2021) *FY21 NIKE, Inc. Impact Report.* [pdf] Available at: https://about.nike.com/en/newsroom/reports/fy21-nike-inc-impact-report-2 [Accessed 23 April 2025].

Nike (2022) *FY22 NIKE, Inc. Impact Report.* [pdf] Available at: https://about.nike.com/en/impact-resources/fy22-nike-inc-impact-report [Accessed 23 April 2025].

Performance Measurement And Management (n.d.) *The Sustainability Strategy Map (Part 1 of 2).* Available at: https://www.pm2consulting.com/post/the-sustainability-strategy-map-par-1-of-2 [Accessed 23 April 2025].

Reinaldo, F. (2020) Nike: Just do it. Differently!. *Harvard Business School Digital Initiative*, 30 April. Available at: https://digital.hbs.edu/platform-digit/submission/nike-just-do-it-differently/ [Accessed 23 April 2025].

RFID Label (2025) Nike Implements Blockchain for Supply Chain Data Collection. Available at:https://www.rfidlabel.com/nike-implements-blockchain-for-supply-chain-data-collection/ [Accessed 23 April 2025].

Seth, C. (2020) 'For Once, Don't Do It': The Powerful Idea Behind Nike's New Anti-Racism Ad. *Forbes,* 30 May. Available at: https://www.forbes.com/sites/sethcohen/2020/05/30/

for-once-dont-do-it---the-powerful-idea-behind-nikes-new-anti-racism-ad [Accessed 23 April 2025].

Shoshy,C. (2021) Nike Acquires Virtual Sneaker Creator RTFKT as It Pushes Deeper Into the Metaverse. *Footwear News Online,*13 December. Available at: https://footwearnews.com/business/mergers-acquisitions/nike-acquires-rtfkt-virtual-sneaker-creator-metaverse-1203220393/#:~:text=Nike%20Inc.%20said%20late%20today%20that%20it%20has,its%20influence%20in%20the%20metaverse%20via%20virtual%20sneakers. [Accessed 22 April 2025].

Sophie, P. (2021) Nike Has Paid No Federal Income Taxes for the Past Three Years. *Willamette Week*, 3 April. Available at: https://www.wweek.com/news/business/2021/04/03/nike-has-paid-no-federal-income-taxes-for-the-past-three-years/ [Accessed 22 April 2025].

Statista (2024) *Nike's revenue worldwide from the fiscal years of 2016 to 2024, by sales channel.*[online] Available at: https://www.statista.com/statistics/888725/nikes-revenue-by-sales-channel-worldwide/ [Accessed 22 April 2025].

Statista (2024) *Nike's revenue worldwide from the fiscal years of 2017 to 2024, by region.* [online] Available at: https://www.statista.com/statistics/241692/nikes-sales-by-region-since-2007/ [Accessed 22 April 2025].

Statista (2024) *Revenue share of Nike worldwide in the fiscal year of 2024, by product category.* [online] Available at: https://www.statista.com/statistics/412760/nike-global-revenue-share-by-product/#:~:text=In%20fiscal%202024%2C%20footwear%20accounted%20for%2068%20percent,notified%20via%20email%20when%20this%20statistic%20is%20updated [Accessed 22 April 2025].

Statista (2025) *Revenue from footwear segment of Nike adidas and Puma from 2010 to 2024.* [online] Available at: https://www.statista.com/statistics/278834/revenue-nike-adidas-puma-footwear-segment/ [Accessed 22 April 2025].

Stephen, G. (2021) Nike and Skechers Settle Three Patent Suits. *Footwear News*, 23 November. Available at: https://footwearnews.com/2021/business/legal-news/nike-skecherssettle-three-patent-lawsuits-1203213489/#:~:text=In%20September%20 2019%2C%20Nike%20filed,Max%20270%20and% 20VaporMax%20designs. [Accessed 22 April 2025].

Stock Analysis (2025) *Nike Inc., (NKE).* Available at: https://stockanalysis.com/stocks/nke/metrics/revenue-by-segment [Accessed 28 April 2025].

Sustainalytics (2024) Company ESG Risk Ratings. 13 November. Available at: https://www.sustainalytics.com/esg-rating/nike-inc/1008170227 [Accessed 22 April 2025].

Sustainable Brands (2013) Nike Partners With Bluesign Technologies To Scale Access To Sustainable Textile. 18 March. Available at: https://sustainablebrands.com/read/nike-partners-with-bluesign-technologies-to-scale-access-to-sustainable-textiles [Accessed 22 April 2025].

Supply Chain Digital (2022) Robots support Nike's supply chain logistics. 31 January. Available at: https://supplychaindigital.com/logistics/robots-support-nikes-supply-chain-logistics [Accessed 22 April 2025].

Tim, S. (2020) What Is a Value Chain Analysis? 3 Steps. *Harvard Business School Online,* 3 December. Available at: https://online.hbs.edu/blog/post/what-is-value-chain-analysis [Accessed 22 April 2025].

Vicky, X.X., James, L. (2020) Your favorite Nikes might be made from forced labor. Here's why. The *Washington Post,* 17 March. Available at: https://www.washingtonpost.com/opinions/2020/03/17/your-favorite-nikes-might-be-made-forced-labor-heres-why [Accessed 22 April 2025].

Wikipedia (2025) Nike Sweatshops. 18 April. Available at: https://en.wikipedia.org/wiki/Nike_sweatshops [Accessed 22 April 2025].

Wikipedia (2025) Just Do It. 17 April. Available at: https://en.wikipedia.org/wiki/Just_Do_It [Accessed 22 April 2025].

Wikipedia (2025) Nike, Inc.30 April. Available at: https://en.wikipedia.org/wiki/Nike,_Inc. [Accessed 22 April 2025].

Wikipedia (2024) Higg Index. 11 November. Available at: https://en.wikipedia.org/wiki/Higg_Index [Accessed 22 April 2025].

Wikipedia (2025) Nike Cortez. 3 April. Available at: https://en.wikipedia.org/wiki/Nike_Cortez [Accessed 22 April 2025].

Wondershare Edrawmind (n.d.) *Nike Market Segmentation, Targeting, and Positioning*. Available at: https://www.edrawmind.com/article/nike-market-segmentation-targeting-and-positioning.html [Accessed 22 April 2025].

Yahoo!Finance (2025) *Nike, Inc. (NIKE).* Available at: https://finance.yahoo.com/quote/NKE/financials/ [Accessed 22 April 2025].

Yahoo!Finance (2025) *Nike, Inc. (NIKE).* Available at: https://finance.yahoo.com/quote/NKE/balance-sheet/ [Accessed 22 April 2025].